Virtual Instruction Standards:
Optimizing Teaching & Learning

National Virtual Teacher Association

Virtual Instruction Standards: Optimizing Teaching & Learning

A Product of the National Virtual Teacher Association

ISBN: 9798555506481
Austin, TX

Virtual Instruction Standards: Optimizing Teaching & Learning

Preface

The National Virtual Teacher Association (NVTA) was created to address the evolving needs of students, educators, and schools. The NVTA worked with a group of veteran virtual instructors across the country, each bringing a unique perspective based on the demographics of the students they instruct, to develop a set of common standards for virtual instruction that are nationally recognized. Based on research and best practices, these standards are built to address all learners and learning environments. These standards will be shared with you in this book. Furthermore, if you are looking to create a virtual program in P-12 or higher education and would like to access the actual rubrics to help set the expectation for high-quality virtual instruction, we encourage you to download them for free at virtualteacherassociation.org.

Our mission is to inspire virtual teachers to provide excellent instruction and our vision is to create a world where virtual teaching is more effective than in-person instruction. In order to achieve this goal, we believe schools must invest in their teachers and teachers must invest in themselves to develop 21st-century skills to create a dynamic virtual learning environment that can meet and even exceed the current in-class experience.

Teachers and Assistants

A high-quality virtual learning environment is different than creating a physical one. The interactions with students are digital, the ability to engage them is substantively varied, and creating assessments and homework that ensure students can learn the content is a significant challenge. To transition to a virtual classroom, teachers and administrators need to acquire new skills and build a common language to build trust. If you're prepared to continue improving your skills and abilities as a virtual instructor or administrator, our online training would be a great companion program to this book. Not only do we offer a free professional development course, but we also offer a certification course. The certification course, accredited by Adams State College allows you to earn three graduate-level credits and will ensure you are trained to be the most effective and impactful virtual instructor in both P-12 and higher education, nationally.

Administrators

Administrators, we also understand the importance of being able to lead your team with high expectations while offering support systems to ensure they are prepared for success. We urge you to utilize this book, the free rubrics, and the free professional development course to provide your team with the necessary tools for virtual learning with high-yielding results.

You set the tone at your district and your campus. Your investment in your teachers is a reflection of the value you place on high-quality education and for that, you are applauded. Thank you for modeling the importance of continuing education as professionals in order to maximize individual potential. We also encourage you to explore the possibility of furthering that investment by having your teachers complete our certification program.

The Certification Program

The certification program exists to set the bar for what quality virtual instruction looks like and to provide a guide on how to achieve a high performing virtual classroom. When a teacher completes this program they are recognized and credentialed as accomplished educators, most suited to deliver virtual instruction. Certification affords participants the skillsets to master technology, enhance their practice, and become the outstanding 21st-century teacher they are meant to be. This certification is bi-annually renewed to ensure teachers remain current on new strategies and technologies available to enhance their pedagogy. Achieving certification may enable a teacher the opportunity to cultivate and create a new career trajectory that allows them to work remotely in a world where virtual education is one of the fastest-growing industries in the world.

Additionally, the certification will allow educators to standout in a competitive teaching market, as colleges and K-12 institutions continuously move their classes online.

Furthermore, once enrolled in the program, participants will have a textbook, an assigned evaluator who will provide feedback on assignments in each stage, and have access to a discussion board to interact with other participants. Upon completion of the program, participants will earn an accredited certificate and have access to the video library as an ongoing support tool. If you are ready to become a superhero for students and further actualize your potential as a premier educator, then visit virtualteacherassociation.org to register now.

How to Utilize this Book

This book will expand on the "Principles of Virtual Teaching" (PVT) throughout each chapter. The PVT is a set of 22 rubrics utilized to evaluate each Strand of virtual instruction. It is strongly recommended that you download your free copy of the PVT at virtualteacherassociation.org and use it to follow along with the chapters.

Some sections will also include real-life stories of virtual teachers and administrators who excelled within specific indicators. These exemplar stories of earning "Accomplished" on the rubric may help you visualize what high-quality implementation of the criteria may look like in action.

Additionally, you will notice a series of questions at the end of each chapter. In order to fully synthesize the material presented and apply the learning to your professional reality, you must take the time to respond meaningfully and thoughtfully engage in your learning. Just as you would encourage your students to take notes in the margin, draw inferences, and capture areas of clarification, we encourage you to do the same.

Remember, you are invested in this work to ultimately improve your effectiveness as an educator. As a result, your students will benefit. Students are at the heart of everything we do in our professional mission. We want you to be your best because your students deserve it.

Appreciation for Our Team

The NVTA was built by a group of educational leaders who have pioneered the delivery of virtual education in the K-12 and higher ed spaces. We believe that when a virtual teacher is trained properly, they can create a world-class learning environment that engages students in the virtual medium they live in every day. We believe it is time to start focusing on how to be an effective virtual teacher by building a community of educators who want to work as a group to create standards and share quality educational options.

We would like to acknowledge the following team members for their contributions to our innovative, cutting-edge, and world-class curriculum and resources in an effort to develop high-quality virtual teachers: Shanna Ayer, Evan Erdbderg, Shelly Fisher, Dr. Keith Lockwood, and Dr. April Willis. We would also like to thank the following team members for their contributions to the real-life examples provided to illustrate what "Accomplished" virtual learning looks like in online classrooms: Shanna Ayer, Marcy Carruth, Catherine Crabtree, Shelly Fisher, Maria Hellard, Aron Hill, Dr. Keith Lockwood, Jason Lynch, Dustin Mathias, and John Rollack Jr.

At the very core of our team is our diverse Education Advisory Board of talented professionals who have a vested interest in improving the quality of professional education. The Education Advisory Board consists of leaders, scholars, and innovators from around the country with extensive knowledge of the importance of quality virtual instruction. The Education Advisory Board is responsible for providing oversight and guidance to the processes by which the NVTA develops guidelines for quality virtual teaching, oversight of the National Virtual Teacher Association Certification, and any other program or innovative curriculum materials that are developed and administered by the NVTA.

We would like to acknowledge the following advisory board members for their dedication and support in building a top-tier virtual certification program: Dr. Sheila Harriosn-Williams, Kimberley Harrington Markus, Dr. Tony Smith, Clifton Taulbert, and Evan Erdberg.

Overview: Principles of Virtual Teaching (PVT)

For more than a decade, school districts have focused on building valid teacher observation systems to help promote a distinguished level of classroom instruction. The real focus on finding a quality instructional observation rubric started with The Measures of Effective Teaching (MET) project, funded by the Bill and Melinda Gates Foundation was designed to inform teachers about the effectiveness of their methods/practices and to help districts identify and develop great teaching.

This was further supercharged with the Race to the Top, a multi-billion dollar U.S. Department of Education competitive grant program under Secretary of Education, Arne Duncan in 2009. Race to the Top was established to support K-12 education reform and innovation in state and local districts. The race was on and using data from the MET study, states and thousands of districts adopted new observation systems and rubrics to measure the quality of instruction. The ultimate goal was to coach and mentor teachers to eventually earn the distinguished rating.

Fast forward seven years later and we are in the era of virtual instruction with access to computers, powerful mobile devices, apps, and online complimentary educational programs. Couple this with recent headline-grabbing studies suggesting iGeneration's attention spans have shrunk to eight seconds and they are unable to focus for extended amounts of time. This creates a new challenge for teachers, especially in the virtual environment where you are not able to control what the student searches for, looks at, listens to, etc. The teacher needs to be highly dynamic and engaging to capture student attention and maintain a steady pace for student learning.

Much of the data and experience that was relied on for creating observation systems to measure teacher effectiveness in the physical classroom did not translate to the virtual classroom. A distinguished teacher rating in the physical classroom may translate to a basic teacher rating in the virtual classroom. In order to set up a distinguished virtual classroom, a teacher needs to learn a whole new set of skills to ensure the iGeneration stays engaged.

This is where NVTA comes in. NVTA recognized that virtual teachers were being evaluated according to in-person instructional expectations and not accounting for virtual variables (e.g., virtual questioning techniques, use of technology, virtual environment preparedness, virtual classroom management, etc.). In order to close the gap between evaluation criteria and virtual instruction effectiveness, a new set of evaluation tools needed to be developed.

NVTA decided to follow virtual instructors around the country, interview parents & students, and interview school &

company administrators who were on the cutting edge of virtual instruction. The ultimate goal was to determine what works and what does not work in virtual instruction. As a result, a team of talented educators and researchers at NVTA created The Principles of Virtual Teaching (PVT) as a common language all teachers, schools, districts, and states could adopt to set expectations and evaluate the effectiveness of virtual instruction.

In this book, you will get access to data that has been tested in classrooms over the past 10 years as schools and educational companies pivoted to create a successful virtual environment. The PVT encapsulates the feedback from educational stakeholders to help you navigate the creation of your own successful virtual classroom. These principles will act as your compass and your guiding light to ensure you do not make the same mistakes others have made throughout the years.

The Principles of Virtual Teaching (PVT) include a series of 22 rubrics categorized into five domains. Within each domain, there are several Strands of focus with indicators zeroing in on very specific criteria. Each indicator has an independent rubric including critical criteria and examples. The rubric has four observation levels of instructional application :

Unsatisfactory: *Teacher consistently performs below the established standards; does not meet requirements of the* *job and minimal student learning; significant to severe impact on loss of instruction time/student engagement*

Basic: *Teacher is inconsistent in meeting standards; requires support, quality of student learning questionable; moderate to significant impact on loss of instruction time/student engagement*

Proficient: *Teacher consistently meets the established standards; consistent positive impact on students; little impact on loss of instructional time/student engagement*

Accomplished: *Teacher maintains performance that consistently surpasses established standards; sustains high performance over time, role model to others; no impact on loss of instructional time/student engagement*

Each chapter will review one domain and all of the Strands/indicators within it. Each chapter will also provide clear instructional indicators and examples of each level of instructional application to the correlating rubric. It is strongly recommended that in order to fully understand and apply the rubrics, you download your free copy of the PVT rubrics at virtualteacherassociation.org. This downloadable resource is an easy to read, 27-page, full-color document that dives deep into all five domains and their corresponding strands and indicators. As a reminder, this book is a companion document to the rubrics.

The PVT addresses the following five domains that impact the success of virtual instruction:

- **Domain 1:** Home Instructional Space & Technology
- **Domain 2:** Class Preparation
- **Domain 3:** Content Knowledge & Virtual Instruction
- **Domain 4:** Virtual Learning Environment & Affect
- **Domain 5:** Professional Practices & Responsibilities

No one domain stands alone- it really takes an accomplished educator to understand how to effectively implement the strands and equivalent strands of each domain in order to maximize student learning in the virtual classroom. As you explore each domain and the corresponding strands, you will gain a better understanding of what to focus on when improving your instructional approach. Furthermore, you will read examples of unsatisfactory practices in order to recognize methods to avoid.

Activity Set: Overview

1. What are your top three concerns about excelling as an educator in the virtual environment?

    a. _____

    _____

    b. _____

    _____

    c. _____

    _____

2. What excites you most about being an online teacher?

    _____

    _____

3. I will know this book and the accompanying rubrics add value to my career if:

    _____

    _____

4. I have downloaded the NVTA Principles of Virtual Teaching at virtualteacherassociation.org and will have them readily available while reading this corresponding book in order to make the most of my professional learning experience. _____Yes _____No

NOTES:

Domain 1: Home Instructional Space & Technology

Domain 1 focuses on the teacher's instructional space, presentation, and equipment required for online teaching. Specifically, ensuring these instructional Strands are conducive for conducting live classes with efficiency, effectiveness, and minimal distractions to students. This domain includes two strands, with a total of two indicators which allow an observer to determine their individual level of application:

Strand: Home Instructional Space

A: Instructional Space

Strand: Technology Equipment & Usage

B: Technology Requirement & Equipment

Notice in Domain 1, the environment and equipment are being evaluated on efficiency, effectiveness, and minimal student distraction. While these are subjective, the rubric for each indicator outlines the critical criteria and examples of all levels from "Unsatisfactory" to "Accomplished."

Indicator 1A: Instructional Space

Instructional Space is defined as the teacher's working space, including setup and surroundings, that are compatible with virtual instruction during live classes with students. Let's explore three focal points as they relate to the instructional space.

Background

When teachers are instructing virtually, their video projects not only their cheerful faces/affect, but also anything in the background of their environment. If the background is cluttered or showing inappropriate items/posters/paraphernalia, then students may become distracted (unsatisfactory). Instead, it is strongly encouraged that teachers have, at a minimum, a blank wall (basic). Whereas, they may take it a step further and utilize a green screen to showcase the school logo and images related to the content (proficient). An accomplished teacher may also incorporate the background as an interactive whiteboard teaching tool many times while using the green screen to showcase examples, videos, labs, etc. This background interactivity may increase the engagement of their students which parallels the experience of physically being in-class in front of their students.

Interruptions

Professionalism at home can be challenging, especially if the teacher lives with pets and/or other people. If those pets or people are frequently seen or heard, students will become distracted (unsatisfactory). If the distractions rarely occur, then the teacher is more (basic). However, if the educator can manage to completely remove the distractions of people and pets, then this would contribute to a Proficient rating. When a teacher not only

23

has limited interruptions, but ensures there is a plan for unplanned interruptions including a package delivery, a phone call, young children at home, etc. they have demonstrated themselves to be an accomplished virtual teacher.

Materials

Accomplished teachers ensure the required materials are readily available. However, if they must frequently stop to find materials, reducing the instructional time in front of students or compelling students to sit and wait during class they are (unsatisfactory). If a teacher frequently pauses during class to locate resources resulting in minimal loss of instructional time, they are (basic). In contrast, a proficient teacher has few interruptions as they have allocated their time prior to class to prepare the materials on their own computer and/or uploaded them to the learning management system/video delivery system to ensure a seamless virtual class. An accomplished teacher takes virtual instruction one step further by learning how to auto-populate a students screen during a live class session with the materials they require, by offering custom learning resources for each student. They maximize every instructional minute while the students are in class.

Indicator 1B: Technology Requirement & Equipment

This Strand evaluates the teacher's technology access and equipment. Specifically, it seeks to identify, if the internet connection, software/hardware/monitor, etc. are sufficient and afford the teacher the resource capacity to deliver online instruction during a live class. Let's explore two essential areas as they relate to virtual instruction technology requirements.

Internet

The expectation for virtual instruction is that the student and the teacher can maintain seamless communication through a strong internet connection. While teachers cannot control students' access to the internet or the quality of connection on the student end, teachers are able to control the quality of their personal internet connection. An unsatisfactory rating would be appropriate for a teacher who regularly loses internet connection and makes no attempt to reconnect or proactively inform students what to do if internet connection should fail. A basic rating is earned if a teacher frequently loses connection and is slow to rejoin the class, creating an expectation for their students that class will not always occur which reduces instructional time and student engagement. Proficient teachers rarely have internet connection issues, but if their internet connection fails, they quickly re-enter the classroom. Finally, an accomplished teacher not only rarely has internet issues, but also has a preparedness plan in place for students to follow in case the teacher briefly loses internet access. This can include saved recorded lessons, a hotspot backup, etc. to maximize instructional time for their students, which sets the highest expectation for engagement.

Video Delivery System

Similarly to internet accessibility, video delivery systems (VDS), also known as video conferencing, may encounter software glitches that prohibit a smooth instructional process due to continual updates. Teachers with an unsatisfactory rating may often need to restart their program and/or computer during live class creating a disruption to instructional time. They also utilize minimal features of the VDS. Teachers with a basic proficiency level in VDS will occasionally need to restart their program during live class and use basic value-add features such as grouping students and muting and unmuting students. Teachers rated as proficient will rarely interrupt live class for a restart and will use the enhanced features to increase student participation on a regular basis. Accomplished teachers reflect minimal to non-existent class interruptions to restart their computers or VDS and seamlessly adopt any new features the VDS offers to continue dynamic classroom instruction.

Short Story: An Accomplished Math Teacher from the Virtual Classroom

I was super excited when I found a job where I got to work from home and could still be home with my two-year old. I did not have this opportunity with my oldest two children, so it was such a blessing to get this opportunity now. So, I set up part of my spare bedroom as an office, checked with my internet provider to ensure I had enough bandwidth, and then started teaching. I put my computer at a desk and got to work.

One day, while I was teaching, my daughter walked in and the students started oohing and ahhing. I asked, "What is going on?" One of my students replied, "Mrs. Carruth, your daughter just walked in." I introduced her to the class, and they were excited to meet her. Then, I proceeded to teach again and quickly realized how much time it took to get the students back on task once she left.

At the end of the day, I got to reflecting. What is the best way for my office to be arranged to create the best experience for my students and myself? What other issues was I dealing with that I needed to find a solution for? This is what I came up with.

1. Desk location: I moved my desk so that my back was to a wall where I was across from the door so I could easily see anyone who entered the room. I could quickly mute my mic if I ever needed.

2. Lighting: I had the light overhead that was in the room as well as the window light. During different parts of the day it was either not enough light or too much. I bought a lamp that had 3 light heads on it where I could adjust each one as needed.

3. Tablet: I had been using a mouse to teach math and it was very difficult to write equations clearly with it. I decided to purchase a tablet which helped tremendously in neatness and clarity to my students.

4. Desk: I was used to walking around a room when I taught in a brick and mortar school and once I had a full load of classes virtually I was sitting at a desk all day. I knew this was not good for me so I looked into getting a standing desk. Some teachers purchase these, but at the time did not have the money to do so. As a result, I bought a workbench, which was much cheaper and created my own standing desk with the use of things I had around the house to get the perfect height for my computer.

5.   Dual Monitors: Having 1 screen to see students as well as see the materials I needed to use was difficult. So I decided to have 2 monitors. I had an extra tv in the house so I used it to connect to my computer. This allowed me to see all of my students on 1 screen and all of the materials I was going to use for the day on the other. This allowed for quick transitions between materials I was sharing with the students to ensure no loss of instructional time

6.   Virtual Backgrounds & Green Screen: Being in a classroom, it is easy to use teaching resources such as posters, or other visual aides to help enforce or recall important details from past lessons. By having a virtual background with the resource on it, I was able to do the same. This also gives your students a better presentation of you and gives your surroundings a more polished look. When I used zoom at first, I needed a physical greenscreen up behind me, but with all of the new updates some computers allow you to show a virtual background without the green screen present.

7.   Internet: I checked to ensure I had the highest speeds possible so that there would be no interruption in service when sharing content. I also made sure I had access to a hotspot through my phone in case there was ever an outage with my home internet

service. The hotspot also made it possible for me to teach from anywhere, so I was able to travel and do my job when necessary.

8.   Other Resources: Some teachers purchase a doc camera and connect it to their computers. This allows them to write on paper documents they have in front of them to share with their students. I have found that I personally have never needed to do this because I could just share whatever document I had on my computer and write on it using the annotate feature in Zoom for students to follow along but it is an option some teachers choose to use.

Having a professional work space set up for a virtual classroom is essential to establishing presence, poise, and confidence for all stakeholders.

Activity Set: Home Instructional Space & Technology

1. Identify space in your home that can easily be utilized as a virtual classroom. List the items in the background that may be seen of students

a. _____

b. _____

c. _____

d. _____

2. How will you ensure other people/pets in your home do not interfere with your virtual instruction? Do you have a process in place to communicate with them that your classroom is off-limits during certain times?

_____

_____

_____

3. On a scale of 1-10, how reliable is your internet, with 10 being most reliable? _____

a. What will you do to increase reliability?

_____

4.   What VDS value added feature are you excited to use with a class of students?

_____

_____

_____

NOTES:

Domain 2: Class Preparation

Domain 2 focuses on the teacher's capacity to adequately prepare for a successful virtual learning experience through communication, digital resources, and pacing. In order to evaluate teacher preparation, this domain focuses on two strands, with a total of three indicators:

Strand: Communication & Information

A: Facilitator Communication & Class

Information (Optional)

Strand: Lesson Planning & Resources

B: Lesson Planning & Resources

C: Class Pacing

The importance of preparing for effective communication with a classroom facilitator, becoming familiar with digital resources, and planning for instruction that is consistent with online learning are expanded upon in Domain 2. Additionally, it is important to note that indicator A only applies to virtual educators who are assigned a facilitator. We recognize that not all schools may be in a position to include a facilitator for every teacher. If you do not have a facilitator, you may omit 2A from your practice and concluding evaluation. However, if you do have the added advantage of a classroom facilitator in your virtual instruction, 2A will apply to you.

Indicator 2A: Facilitator Communication & Class Information (Optional- Only if assigned a Facilitator)

Facilitator communication is rated on the teacher's willingness and capacity to contact and communicate procedures with the in-class facilitator. It also may involve the teacher's ability to garner requisite information when planning virtual instruction. Let's explore two coverage areas as they relate to facilitator communication.

Communication Initiative

The difference between an unsatisfactory rating and an accomplished rating is the level of initiative the teacher assumes in communicating with the facilitator:

Unsatisfactory: Initiates little to no communication, severely delays/does not respond to the facilitator, and/or treats the facilitator unprofessionally.

Basic: Teacher initiates occasional communication with delayed responses and demonstrates minimal professional respect for the facilitator.

Proficient: Initiates consistent communication and responds in a timely manner while showing respect for the facilitator. In addition, asks for the facilitator's phone number and email to set up communication. This teacher will arrange monthly meetings with the facilitator.

Accomplished: Initiates ongoing communication with prompt responses. This teacher consistently contacts the facilitator daily and arranges a weekly planning session to pre-plan for the instructional week. The facilitator and the teacher are a well-established team creating a highly effective learning environment. The facilitator knows how each student is performing and by extension is an integral part of the teaching team.

An accomplished teacher may also communicate with the facilitator via text or email during class. Engaging with the facilitator in live class time is the best way to ensure students are receiving the support they need and the facilitator is being utilized effectively.

Class Information: Grading Periods, Policies, and Students

Having a thorough understanding of student behavior is an important aspect to running an effective classroom. Similarly, knowing and implementing school policies and adhering to grading deadlines are critical Strands to ensuring your classroom is well-positioned for success.

When a teacher is completely unaware (unsatisfactory) or mostly unaware (basic) of students who may require significant accommodation in the learning environment or is unaware of policies/procedures, this can adversely affect student learning outcomes. A proficient teacher is mostly aware of students who may require significant accommodation in the learning environment and is mostly aware of policies/procedures. Finally, accomplished teachers are not just fully aware of these critical indicators, but also proactively check in regularly for updates to ensure he/she is always following best practices and creates the most positive learning environment for all students.

Short Story: Middle School Social Studies Teacher

At the beginning of one school year we had an influx of courses come in all at one time and as a result a slew of emails were being sent. It became apparent that the school needed a way to get all departments on the same page. I decided to create a meeting with all departments where we could come together to discuss immediate issues that needed to be addressed.

As I reflect on this time, I realize a bunch of other processes came about as a result. Here is a look at the outcomes.

1.   Communication between departments: We held biweekly meetings which changed to weekly meetings once other processes were put in place. These meetings were used to deal with

immediate issues that needed to be resolved quickly. We implemented Google forms to set up workflows to and from different departments to ensure followup and completion of tasks.

2.   Communication within a department: We set up weekly meetings to discuss current issues that were happening at our schools, as well as, other long term projects that needed to be completed. Also, we utilized Google chat within departments to alert the different members within the group when an issue arose that needed immediate attention.

3.   Training for staff: Asynchronous (async) training was provided to our staff before and during the school year with live office hours available for follow-up conversations. This allowed for a bigger number of employees to be trained on our platforms at a faster pace to ensure the teachers were ready to teach. Teachers were given a set amount of time to complete the training but had the flexibility to do it whenever was best for them. Professional development was provided biweekly based on school feedback and observations we did of our teachers. This PD time allowed for teachers to try new cutting-edge technologies to use with their students to keep them highly engaged.

4. Training for facilitators: Async training was provided for facilitators to complete at their convenience. In addition, teachers were trained to reach out to the facilitators by email before their classes started to get any information that the school wanted them to follow directly from the school. This was also a way for the teacher and facilitator to start to build their working relationship and have an open line of communication.

5. Parent & Student Communication: Teachers are able to use our platform to communicate with their students directly by email on their work or behavior. Furthermore, teachers have access to different application options to communicate with parents and students to quickly inform them about student progress.

By putting these processes in place we were able to train staff quickly and were able to manage large groups of employees effectively. We will continue to implement new processes along the way to ensure we are accomplishing our mission of connecting all learners with the expert teachers they deserve.

Indicator 2B: Lesson Planning & Resources

Lesson planning and resources are essential to an effective lesson. Teachers must know where the lesson is going and what tools will be used to get there. Let's explore three critical focal areas as they relate to lesson planning and resources.

Posting Lesson Plans

Simply not posting lesson plans or posting very basic ones (e.g., "Today we will learn about WWII") is the characteristic of an unsatisfactory teacher. A basic rating is earned if they normally do not post plans or they just state at the beginning of class what they plan for the lesson. However, a proficient rating can be earned if the teacher posts regularly. An accomplished rating is earned if the teacher posts plans regularly and reminds students what they will learn at the beginning of each class period.

Access to Activities

Have you ever seen something demonstrated for you and you just couldn't wait to try it yourself? Students are the same way. When teachers demo activities in class, students are often eager to engage in those activities for themselves. An unsatisfactory rating for a teacher in this capacity does not make activities accessible during class and might only demonstrate it on their computer instead of empowering students to participate. A basic rating means the teacher rarely uses activities to stimulate learning and focuses more on teacher driven instruction during class. A proficient rating means that students are provided multiple types of activities during the class time such as Nearpod or a virtual science lab to create an engaging, student-centered classroom. To achieve an accomplished rating, the teacher provides access to activities during each class session that requires students to learn on their own and participate in their own learning experience.

Resources

Resources enhance the instructional experience. If a teacher only uses resources in the Learning Management System (LMS) or attempts to use resources that aren't compatible with virtual learning, they would earn an unsatisfactory rating. Using minimal outside resources and those mostly found in your LMS reflects a basic rating. Now, proficient ratings can be earned if several virtually compatible resources are used and activities including Quizlet are regularly utilized. When the teacher can incorporate not just outside resources, but gamification resources to excite and engage students during every live class session, he/she earns an accomplished rating.

Short Story: Kindergarten Teacher in Siler City

The headlines read "The Latino Invasion of Siler City." I wasn't completely shocked since Siler City is a very small community of farmers and families who have lived there for generations. The "invasion" was a direct result of the Tyson Chicken Plant's relocation to Siler City and the amount of jobs it offered. However, the educators refused to buy into the negative press associated with hardworking families starting a new life in a town that was less than welcoming. Instead, the Siler City schools launched a dual language program to foster relationships among students who couldn't understand each other. The program began with 18 kindergartens who would remain in the program through the 8th grade.

Effective lesson planning allows time for collaboration and setting high standards for learning expectations, habits, and soft skills across grade levels or courses. When educators are empowered to design learning expectations, curriculum coherence emerges. If teachers are provided with opportunities to collaboratively problem solve and create meaningful lesson plans, they can meet the needs of all learners.

Indicator 2C: Class Pacing

We all learn differently. We cannot assume every child in a class will comprehend every concept at the exact same time or in the same manner. An indicator of a critical and reflective teacher is one who understands how to maximize instructional time, anticipates challenging material or concepts, and is able to maintain pacing goals without impeding student learning. Let's explore three elements of class pacing.

Daily Pacing

Bypassing foundational skills to stay on course is not beneficial for students and will earn a teacher an unsatisfactory rating. Rushing through lessons or skipping activities to make up for lost time is also a poor decision and will earn a teacher a basic rating. Being in a virtual classroom provides a teacher with the option to record each lesson for students to watch again at a later time as well as restructuring the content for individual students according to their pace. As a proficient teacher, you are recording many lessons and focusing on the students who need extra accommodations. If a teacher must hasten lesson pace, he/she is able to discern which activities can be skipped based on student needs during the class session. An accomplished teacher always records every class session, provides individualized materials for each student based on their comprehension of the materials, and understands in advance which activities are not crucial for class/whole group understanding.

Weekly Planning

Due to the many variables in pacing for long-term instruction, curriculum alignment can easily deviate. But, that is precisely why having a well-defined and prepared plan is so important. It is much easier to alter plans that exist than to start from scratch every day. Here are some examples of what longer-term planning may look like for virtual educators:

- Teacher often limits opportunities to practice or allows for student collaboration to make up for lost time, regardless of student understanding (unsatisfactory)
- Teacher plans for a a day or a few days at a time, no plan to address timing issues (basic)
- Teacher has prepared for several weeks in advance and has a general plan to address timing issues (proficient)
- Teacher has prepared for several weeks and anticipates pacing concerns with a well thought out plan (accomplished)

Remediation

We have all been there- the time when it seems like everyone else "gets it" and you just don't know what's happening. It can be a discouraging time when you feel like you're last to catch on, but even more so if you're a student and you feel like you're just not smart enough. Teachers must be equipped to support learners at every stage, which is why remediation strategies are critical for a highly successful teacher. Offering no remediation (unsatisfactory) or few remediation strategies that are not appropriate for the class/student (basic), can have long-lasting negative effects for students. Proficient teachers have remediation resources readily accessible and automatically assign them to each student through the LMS while meeting most students' needs. Going a step further, accomplished teachers would either create a heterogeneously grouped class where they taught the area in need of remediation or create a new lesson for this student. Then, the teacher would both email and attach it to the individual student's profile in the LMS, in addition to providing several more remediation activities to meet ALL student needs.

Activity Set: Class Preparation

1.   Will you have a facilitator? _____ If no, skip to question 2, if yes, draft a communication plan:

a.   Initial Intro: _____

b.   Monthly: _____

c.   Weekly: _____

d.   Daily :_____

2.   List resources you will use to plan lessons and keep grades:

_____

_____

_____

3.   How will you evaluate your ability to pace lessons? What benchmarks will you measure?

_____

_____

_____

NOTES:

Domain 3: Content Knowledge & Virtual Instruction

Domain 3 emphasizes the importance of teachers demonstrating an understanding of content knowledge through the use of current materials and instructional strategies that support students' learning styles, abilities, and objectives in a virtual classroom. In order to evaluate content knowledge and virtual instruction strategies, this domain focuses on two strands, with a total of six indicators:

Strand: Content Knowledge

A: Subject matter expertise

Strand: Instructional Practices

B. Use of Learning Management System & Video Delivery System

C. Innovative Presentation and Teaching with Technology

D. Tiered Learning & Student Grouping

E. Student Questioning

F. Dynamic Instruction

Indicator 3A: Subject Matter Expertise

An effective teacher is able to demonstrate knowledge and understanding of content, materials, and resources appropriate for virtual learning. There are several ways to demonstrate

48

understanding of the content, so let's identify three Strands of teaching that contribute to subject matter expertise.

Responses to Student Questions

Teachers that minimally answer questions (unsatisfactory) or give partial answers (basic) are revealing themselves as someone who doesn't really know what's going on with the material. While teachers aren't expected to know everything all of the time, they are expected to have a certain level of understanding of the material they teach. Proficient teachers are able to respond to student questions and accomplished teachers are able to give very thorough responses to student questions and comments.

Instructional Approaches

Perhaps you're familiar with Gardner's Theory of Multiple Intelligences (1983). The idea is that not every person learns in the same way. Similarly, you may have heard Einstein's quote, "If you judge a fish by its ability to climb a tree, it will live its whole life believing that it is stupid." Educational research tells us that teachers need to utilize a variety of instructional approaches in an attempt to meet the needs of all students. Teachers with an unsatisfactory rating may use limited instructional approaches, relying on 1-2 approaches and activities.

Teachers with a basic rating may utilize limited instructional approaches and rely heavily on LMS activities. Now, teachers identified as proficient may use multi-pronged instructional approaches, both within LMS/VDS and utilizing external resources. An accomplished teacher utilizes a wide variety of approaches and resources that deepens students' critical understanding. Many of the methodologies teachers are using at the accomplished level reflect didactic online resources, quizzes, games, etc., all in order to construct a dynamic curriculum.

Making Connections

Applying new material to the real world not only makes learning more relevant, but it makes learning more fun. When students ask, "When will I ever use this?" Teachers must be able to respond in a way that encourages the student to *want* to learn more. When minimal connections are made (unsatisfactory) or they are very loosely made to prior content or knowledge (basic), students may become disengaged. It is more beneficial if teachers can make solid connections to prior learning (proficient), but the best if teachers can connect the material to multiple subjects, both in and outside of class (accomplished).

Short Story: An Instructional Coach

If you can reach them, you can teach them. That is something I firmly believe and make it a driving force behind working with our nation's youth daily. A highly effective teacher knows their students. They build connections and rapport with them. During remote learning, teachers have had to change the way they reach their kids and keep them engaged. They are the same ideas and principles as in a brick-and-mortar building, however more difficult and challenging. You have the issue of compliance vs. engagement. Some students may log-in and "be there" and others "actively participate." A great teacher works to make sure each student is engaged and given the opportunity to grow.

Highly-effective teachers are masters in their content and pedagogy. They work to make connections between their subject matter and real-world scenarios. They use current events and students' personal experiences to help drive class discussions to relate to the content they are teaching. For example, in literature, students can compare characters in stories to real-life people/things and use textual evidence to make their case.

Teachers are also using online learning programs including NewsELA, which has articles based on current topics for students to read, analyze the text, and respond to questions. The complexity of the text is based on their lexile level. Students work on their current reading level with the goal to continue to increase it and work with more challenging texts as the year progresses. In English language arts or social studies, teachers may also use lyrics conveying a message or theme aligned to a piece of literature they are reading. Students can compare and contrast the two texts and have rich discussions based on the similarities and differences between the two.

Teachers are also able to differentiate and have students work collaboratively in a shared space. Through Microsoft Teams for example, a teacher may use breakout rooms with pre-selected groups and students assigned to work together. Those groups can be same level students (homogenous) working in different tiers or they can be a mixed group of different abilities (heterogenous). All in all, teachers across America, especially in my district and in my building, are working tirelessly to plan and implement lessons which foster student engagement and self-regulated learning. They are working daily with an exorbitant amount of effort and passion to ensure academic, social, and emotional learning of their students is happening. They are doing a tremendous job.

Indicator 3B: Use of Learning Management System (LMS) & Video Delivery System (VDS)

The virtual teacher must be able to successfully navigate and utilize features of the LMS and VDS in order to deliver high-quality virtual learning. Additionally, by effectively using LMS and VDS, the teacher will be able to facilitate student understanding and engagement at a higher level. There are three Strands worth investing in regarding the use of LMS and VDS.

Technical Proficiency

Technology can be immensely beneficial most of the time, but when glitches occur, it can be quite frustrating. One way to minimize technical errors is to practice! The more comfortable you are with technology, the easier it is to troubleshoot errors or predict when problems may occur. An unsatisfactory rating may be given when the teacher fails to make app updates or publish assignments/materials, because they are most likely uncomfortable with using such technology. Basic ratings are for those teachers who are slightly more comfortable with technology, but who still experience technical issues with audio settings or active links. When a teacher develops proficiency, they have very few issues with LMS/VDS and are able to quickly resolve their problems with minimal distraction. When issues are rare and solutions are quickly implemented with no disruption to the class, that is the signature of an accomplished teacher.

Tools & Features

LMS and VDS offer a wealth of opportunities when it comes to utilizing features, resources, and tools. Rarely using a second monitor or discussion board, or checking email may result in the teacher earning an unsatisfactory rating. Occasionally using 1-2 features (e.g., chat, screen share, breakout rooms), but not resulting in increased student engagement, means the teacher would qualify for a basic rating. Proficient ratings are given to those who use a variety of tools, although they may not always enhance student understanding. Accomplished ratings are assigned to those who utilize a wide range of tools AND they facilitate student understanding and engagement.

Seeks Support When Needed

Asking for help isn't always easy. However, when student learning is at stake, then teachers must be able set ego aside and admit when they need assistance utilizing technology. We are charged with creating extraordinary learning opportunities for students and that responsibility must be accepted with a profound sense of responsibility. An unsatisfactory rating would be given to a teacher who does not seek help and/or ignores suggestions from others. Slightly better, but still problematic is the basic rating assigned to those who do not seek help, but waits until a problem requires others to help resolve it. The proficient teacher seeks out help when needed and is open to help and suggestions from others. However, the pinnacle of seeking support, is not only seeking a wide variety of LMS/VDS support resources, but also sharing them with others (accomplished).

Short Story: Special Education Teachers in a Hybrid Classroom
As I opened the art-covered door to the elementary resource room on a school visit last spring, I got my first glimpse into the magic. Students from 2nd-5th grade reciting new words together in small groups, practicing math manipulatives with a partner, and lying under their desks with a book. As I circulated through the room and talked to these eager young learners it became clear what these Accomplished teachers had leveraged here. By using Zoom breakout rooms and taking advantage of the physical space of the students' classroom, these Special Education teachers had created hybrid stations which students could engage with throughout the lesson. Small groups learned new material and practiced new skills with their teacher while partners did a guided, hands-on

activity together, and individual students read independently and assessed their comprehension using online quizzes.

In live virtual instruction, it is tempting to want to leverage all the latest and greatest digital tools. However, while these new tools are powerful, Accomplished teachers also remember that a strong virtual teacher works to implement those tried and true educational practices that teachers have turned to for years.

Hybrid stations create dynamic environments which increase student engagement, allow students to transition authentically between skills and create more opportunities for individualized interventions. Effective virtual teachers make time for movement, seek ways for students to use their senses, and allow them to take ownership of their own learning.

Indicator 3C: Innovative Presentation & Teaching with Technology

Virtual learning can only be successful if the teacher understands how to best utilize technology. They need to have a thorough understanding of when to use the appropriate features to support student learning, understanding, and engagement. They must also be willing to try new things as innovative technology is always coming out. There are three main Strands regarding innovative presentation and teaching with technology.

Background

As previously mentioned in 1A, the background needs to be appropriate for virtual instruction. Here is a summary of ratings based on teacher backgrounds:

Unsatisfactory: Background is of a messy kitchen or family members can be frequently seen

Basic: Background shows the agenda from two days ago or is too brief to give clarity

Proficient: Background shows the day's agenda and has information related to the current instruction

Accomplished: Background thoroughly informs students of the day's activities and needed materials; includes additional information that allows students to engage or deepen their understanding. The teacher uses their background to lead instruction.

Materials & Features

Knowing how to share your screen during virtual learning or how to use breakout rooms for collaboration are critical tech skills for the classroom. An example of an unsatisfactory rating would be not utilizing screen share or a document camera when working on math problems. A basic rating would be using one of those features, but not the most appropriate one for any given situation. A proficient teacher knows how to use appropriate features, but may rely heavily on 1- 2 features only. The accomplished teacher can use multiple features, materials, and interactive activities to engage students and reinforce learning.

Organization of Materials

An effective learning environment includes an organized LMS. When the layout of the LMS makes locating information difficult with links to assignments missing/broken (unsatisfactory) or the organization of materials is inconsistent (basic), then learning is compromised. On the other hand, when organization is consistent and links work (proficient), students will be set-up for a successful learning experience. Furthermore, when the materials in LMS are well organized and links consistently function properly (accomplished), then the teacher and students are all better off.

Short Story: An Accomplished Teacher from the Virtual Classroom, Ms. Fisher, 11th Grade English Language Arts

Expert teaching in the virtual classroom requires more than tech-savviness and proficiency with learning management systems and video conferencing tools. There is simply no replacement for responsive teaching, relationship building, and authentic communication.

"Okay guys, good work this morning. This is a great close to our group research paper. Thank you for working in some of the tools from your writing rubric. I appreciate that so many of you contributed this week. Let's take all that we have talked about and make it happen in your individual papers today. It's all about the powerful close and leaving your reader with something to think about. Remember, send me a "3" in chat if you're good to go and just need some time to work. Send me a "2" if you want to go over what we talked about this morning one more time in a small group. And, send me a "1" if you'd like to talk to me one-on-one before you get started. Look forward to seeing y'all in breakout rooms." Ms. Fisher scanned the chat quickly and assigned breakout rooms. She was happy to see that one of her students who had been absent for a week had sent her a "1."

"Hi Shawna, how are you? I have missed you!"

Shawna slowly looked at the camera, worried about her teacher's response. "I was suspended."

Ms. Fisher smiled reassuringly. "I am sorry that you went through that. I hope you're okay."

Shawna's mood brightened. "I sent you a '1' because I am behind. Do I have time to catch up on my paper?"

"You surely do! Tell me about your topic. What occupation are you researching for your future career?"

"I am starting a business to help people. I want to show them what they can do and all they can be."

Expert virtual educators leverage digital resources not only to ensure non-negotiable pedagogy in the learning environment, but also to provide responsive teaching, productive relationships, and effective communication that students deserve. The implications are far-reaching and go well beyond student success in their virtual classroom.

Indicator 3D: Tiered Learning & Student Grouping

Just as in an in-person classroom, students in the virtual setting will learn at different rates. This will require tiered instruction and ability-level student grouping. However, in the virtual classroom, meeting the needs of every student can be challenging if the teacher is not prepared for digital tiered instruction. There are two main Strands to meeting these requirements: assignment options and student grouping.

Assignment Options

When students are all given the same assignments in the LMS, regardless of their abilities or levels, or are given only one opportunity to demonstrate mastery of the learning objectives (unsatisfactory), then we are failing to meet the needs of every student. Even if they are inconsistently given one or two choices with a few opportunities to demonstrate mastery of the learning objectives (basic), we are still providing inadequate instruction for every student. On the other hand, when students are allowed to choose their practice and assessment options and are occasionally given multiple attempts to demonstrate mastery (proficient), then the teacher exerts a solid attempt to meet the needs of all students. Consequently, encouraging students to create their own assessments in the LMS and assignments using a rubric, AND having multiple opportunities to demonstrate mastery (accomplished) means that we have thoroughly met every student's individual instructional needs, and are giving them the best chance at being successful without compromising rigor.

Student Grouping

Part of the learning process is explaining what you know to others. It is also hearing someone else's interpretation of content. Engaging in academic conversations/Socratic discussions and defending theories can only occur when students have the opportunity to collaborate with each other. Within a virtual classroom, grouping students is a feature all teachers can use to invigorate learning, but they have to be willing to learn how this feature works. Students who are never given the chance to work together (unsatisfactory) are missing an essential Strand of the learning process. Though they have limited opportunities to work together, especially when groups are mismatched or chosen on the spot without regard to ability levels or student roles (basic), then again, we are providing a subpar learning environment. It is only when students often have opportunities to collaborate in groups purposefully arranged based on performance in the last assessment with student-led roles and frequent teacher guidance (proficient) when we can finally see the positive results of student grouping and the learning process. When roles and activities in regularly occurring ability-level groups are student-led and the teacher pre-assigns the flexible groups based on collective data (accomplished), then students will be able to maximize the results of virtual learning with peer collaboration.

Short Story: An Accomplished Teacher from the Virtual Classroom, 11th grade English Language Arts Teacher

"Ms. Fisher, may I read my paper to you?" The student's eyes were eager and hopeful as they watched the screen intently.

"Dear Ms. Fisher, thank you for being our teacher this year. You helped me do things that I never thought I could..." The student stopped there because she couldn't finish her letter. She had started to cry.

Ms. Fisher had teared up as well. "Thank you so much! Thank you so much for those kind words! I have enjoyed being your teacher this year very much!" The normally firm and structured assistant in the classroom struggled with her own emotions as well and explained that every single student had written a letter to their teacher. One by one, they each read to Ms. Fisher and told her how she had made a difference to them.

As they read, Ms. Fisher recalled her first day with them. She had worried, "How will I ever establish a rapport with them online?" She thought back to her use of breakout rooms and how the teacher's assistant had marveled at the students' respectful, but pointed debates while interpreting classical poems in collaborative groups. She was amazed at how they had risen to Ms. Fisher's high expectations and worked so hard for her the entire year. Ms. Fisher had named that particular unit of study, "Writing like Whitman," but most of the students had chosen to write like Langston Hughes, Emily Dickinson, or Lewis Carroll.

One student in particular, had asked for a one-on-one breakout room session with Ms. Fisher because he wanted to write like Langston Hughes, but he wasn't sure what his topic should be. After listening intently to him explain, Ms. Fisher had offered a suggestion. "Langston Hughes was a very brave individual. He wrote about topics that were very timely, but not very popular and he told the truth about how it felt to live during desegregation. Is there something happening right now to you and your friends? Something that might not be easy to write about maybe?"

"Bullying. It happens every day to a lot of us." That day, the writing conference was as much about ways to stay safe as it was grammar, literary tools, and rhyme & meter.

As she watched the students and listened to their carefully penned words of gratitude, she knew their time with her in breakout rooms studying the classics, reflecting on their areas of need, setting goals for their year, and working with peers collaboratively would serve them well in their chosen careers. She also knew that

she would never forget them.

Indicator 3E: Student Questioning

Assessing student learning through questioning is a key driver in formative assessment. Using online resources gives teachers many unique ways to engage students using topics and games they enjoy to stimulate higher engagement. Using online resources, teachers can quickly evaluate which students are following along, which ones are ahead of the class, and which ones require scaffolding. In order to draw those conclusions, the teacher must ask appropriate questions framed to facilitate students thinking in a virtual setting. Let's explore the three main Strands of student questioning and remember, it's about how teachers apply these Strands effectively in a virtual classroom.

Bloom's Taxonomy of Questions

Bloom's Taxonomy (1956) is a model used to assess the complexity and specificity of learning. It is a hierarchical system in which the highest level of learning occurs at the top of a pyramid with the most fundamental learning serving as the base of the pyramid. This framework consists of six major categories:

Knowledge, Comprehension, Application, Analysis, Synthesis, and Evaluation. If a teacher uses only the most basic level of questioning that only requires students to respond in simplistic recall or rote memorization, then that would earn an unsatisfactory rating. If the teacher asks questions that would be classified as knowledge, comprehension, and/or application, then they would earn a basic rating. When questions increase in rigor to application and/or analysis, the teacher would be rated proficient. Finally, the teacher questioning routinely is categorized as analysis, synthesis, and evaluation, that teacher would earn a rating of accomplished.

Learning Opportunities

Teachable moment opportunities are not often planned. These are those rare moments when students make an observation and have a desire to learn more about the situation. When teachers do not take advantage of those opportunities and only provide simplistic answers (unsatisfactory), then they have lost a substantial moment of learning for students. Sometimes teachers may utilize those teachable moments, but only for a few students and not at the depth they could have pursued (basic). When teachers really do take advantage of the teachable moment, extend that learning to much of the class, and begin to guide students in critical thinking processes (proficient) then we start to see positive results with learning opportunities. Furthermore, when the teacher actively guides critical-thinking processes for the whole class and consistently provides resources 'to support lower-level students (accomplished) then that learning opportunity is fully maximized.

Student Engagement

It can be hard to teach when students aren't paying attention. It can also be difficult to learn when students are distracted. Maintaining student engagement can be a challenge in the virtual classroom, but with the right lesson, instructional strategies, and effective behavior management techniques, student engagement is within reach. Here is how student engagement can affect your teacher rating:

Unsatisfactory: Most students off-task and not paying attention

Basic: Several students paying attention, but most are off-task

Proficient: Many students paying attention and actively engaged

Accomplished: Most or all students are actively engaged and paying attention

Indicator 3F: Dynamic Instruction

Dynamic instruction means that the teacher provides effective instruction and learning activities that support clear objectives and learning goals in a virtual environment. The teacher is able to modify instruction and questioning techniques based on student responses identified needs in the LMS. There are two leading Strands of dynamic instruction: lesson planning and lesson delivery.

Lesson Planning

Best practice has demonstrated that prominently displaying the lesson plan objectives on the screen when students login promotes focused instruction and helps students understand what their goals are for the day. When lesson plans are missing objectives and students become disengaged without a learning target (unsatisfactory) or the lesson objective is very vague with activities misaligned to the objectives (basic), student learning will diminish. However, when teachers have clear objectives supported by meaningful activities (proficient) or previous lesson extension by reinforcing prior objectives with clearly aligned activities (accomplished), learning time for students will be optimized.

Lesson Delivery

Remember when we discussed the multiple intelligences theory in a previous section? Although there are auditory learners, most people don't prefer to sit in a lecture for an extended period of time, especially students. Their bodies were meant to move and to discover learning through exploring curiosities. Teachers who lecture for a long period of time with few breaks (unsatisfactory) or who do not chunk material into smaller portions and seldom offer breaks (basic) may lose student engagement. When lessons have 1-2 instructional methods or activities that cater to a variety of learning styles with breaks for movement and discussion (proficient), then we have begun to embark upon a learning experience that will result positively for most students. If a teacher can use multiple instructional methods and activities that meet the needs of all learning styles and gives adequate breaks for movement and discussion (accomplished), then students in that virtual classroom have been thoroughly prepared for success.

Activity Set: Content Knowledge & Virtual Instruction

1.   Do you believe you are a subject matter expert (SME) in the areas you teach? _____ Circle the following options that you plan on pursuing to continue increasing your knowledge in order to be the most prepared virtual instructor you can be:

a.   Earn another degree

b.   Earn another certification

c.   Attend a state/national conference

d.   Present content to peers

e.   Join a book club in your content area

f.   Other: _____

2.   Draft a list of higher-order thinking verbs using Bloom's Taxonomy (e.g., create, build, simulate, etc.)

_____

_____

_____

3.   Practice using each feature of the VDS your school utilizes. Which features are uncomfortable for you and how will you improve your proficiency with them?

_____

_____

_____

4. Practice using the features of the LMS your school utilizes. Which features are uncomfortable for you and how will you improve your proficiency with them?

_____

_____

_____

NOTES:

Domain 4: Virtual Learning Environment & Affect

Domain 4 emphasizes the importance of teachers demonstrating a positive attitude and tone that facilitates a successful learning environment, encouraging both students and facilitators. In order to evaluate the virtual learning environment and affect, this domain focuses on two strands, with a total of four indicators:

Strand: Affect

A: Student Relationships

B. Facilitator Relationships

C. Student Engagement & Motivation

Strand: Teacher Engagement

D. Teacher Support & Availability

Indicator 4A: Student Relationships

Teachers who demonstrate a positive and professional attitude can facilitate supportive student relationships and success in a virtual classroom. Building those relationships upfront can make the learning environment so much more productive because students trust you and believe that you are there for their best interests. Regarding student relationships, there are three Strands we will investigate.

Student Disruptions

It is expected that at some point, student disruptions will occur in even the most engaging classes, with the most beloved teachers. This is acutely prevalent in a virtual environment since the students are not in a controlled classroom. Students are able to browse to different websites, turn the camera off, become engaged in a conversation with family or friends, use their phones, etc. all which can lead to disruptions. How teachers respond to these interruptions reflects on their ability to cultivate positive relationships with students. For example, if a teacher often gets harsh, loses their temper, shouts at disruptive students, and/or just turns their camera and microphone off without addressing the issue so the student can have the opportunity to correct their mistake (unsatisfactory), then they will likely continue to experience continual disruptions from a variety of students who feel dismissed and marginalized. If a teacher spends time lecturing the class on good behavior and sometimes shuts off a student's microphone or video instead of trying to alter their behavior to rejoin the class successfully (basic), they will still be burdened with regular student disruptions because the relationship just isn't there. In a virtual classroom, the teacher has the option to mute disruptive students and continue demonstrating a cheerful affect by positively educating students or taking time to group the students to focus on the students not engaged directly (proficient), which keeps the rest of the class engaged and positive about the learning experience. The most accomplished teachers are able to actually refocus the disruptive students and involve them in the lesson in an assuring way; they might even reach out to the student's parents and refocus the attention away from the distraction to re-engage the students.

Student Debriefing

After a major disruption, there will likely be a debrief call with the teacher and an administrator. On this call, if the teacher spends most of the time venting and even using inappropriate language (unsatisfactory) and spends little time brainstorming possible future solutions or offering any examples of the behavior (basic), then the teacher will continue to struggle with student relationships. The teacher is the adult in this situation and is tasked with generating creative, proactive ways to support even the most difficult students. A proficient teacher might handle a debriefing call with a professional demeanor, providing data-based observations, video clips from the class, or discussion board examples from the student and brainstorm constructive solutions for the parent. An accomplished teacher doesn't have to debrief about student disruptions because there are none. The teacher quickly re-engages students and maintains high behavior standards that students are willing to follow due to their positive relationship with the teacher. If they need to have a discussion, they have video clips of the student's behavior with scripted measures on how to turn this around. Quite often, this teacher will work with the student after hours to re-engage them.

Student Responses

In a virtual classroom, interacting with students looks a little different than in a traditional classroom. A less experienced teacher may feel overwhelmed and keep all students on mute, most of the time (unsatisfactory). This prevents the teacher from cultivating positive relationships with students. A teacher with a basic rating would mute most students and only interact with the ones who demonstrate interest. A proficient teacher would congratulate students when they answered questions correctly and not overuse the mute button. They would also create a reward system and look to use outside resources to encourage student engagement (e.g., tokens, Quizlet, etc.). An accomplished teacher ensures that all students are so actively engaged in the lesson that they ask for additional learning opportunities. They are using dynamic online resources with pictures, videos, and culturally specific examples along with gamification to drive 90-100% engagement during every class. Their methods will empower even shy students to participate in the virtual class through these systems.

Short Story: An Accomplished Teacher from the Virtual Classroom, Mrs. D, High School Math

Mrs. D has the "Do First" assignment posted on her s colorful and welcoming screen. Everything is prepared so that she can focus on her incoming students.

"Good morning Alana, how are you today?"
"Good morning Jordan, how'd the game go last night?"
"Hi Sam, nice to see you!"
"Good morning Roberto, I responded to your Canvas message about the homework- let me know if you have other questions!"

In just the first 2 minutes of class, 24 private Zoom chats go out, one to each of her students. Almost every student responds and begins their "Do First" warm-up. It was so simple and yet so effective.

When students were later asked about their experience with online math in high school, here is how they responded:
"It's really hard, but I know Mrs. D will help me."
"I feel comfortable asking Mrs. D for help."
"Mrs. D is one of the nicest teachers I have. I was worried an online teacher would be like a robot."

"I actually look forward to this class- Mrs. D plays games with us and they've helped me learn more this year than in the past."

Whether online or in-person, being a great teacher is all about making connections. Mrs. D's commitment to connecting with her students fostered an environment where students felt safe and supported enough to pursue learning in a virtual setting.

Indicator 4B: Facilitator Relationships (Optional)

If your classroom will operate with a facilitator, then cultivating that relationship is equally important. This person will support you and the students and should be treated courteously and acknowledged as a professional. If your classroom does not have a facilitator, you may skip this section and go to indicator 4C. This section will explore three Strands of building a positive facilitator relationship.

Relationship

Demonstrating a positive and professional attitude is the first step in building a positive relationship with your facilitator. Effectively communicating and collaborating leads to classroom success for your students. A teacher with an unsatisfactory rating would have minimal communication with the facilitator due to the lack of effort and cooperation on behalf of the teacher. If the teacher seldom contacts the facilitator for any issues or concerns, then the teacher would earn a basic rating. When the relationship is generally positive, but the facilitator has little voice in classroom procedures, the teacher would earn a proficient rating. When the relationship is positive and effective because both the teacher and the facilitator have an active part in class decision making, then the teacher would earn an accomplished rating. The teacher drives the relationship with the facilitator and that's why it is so important to put forth the effort in creating a positive relationship that will result in a more cooperative classroom and better support for students.

Collaboration

The facilitator and teacher work together to create a high-quality classroom. If the teacher does not allow the facilitator to have a voice (unsatisfactory) or to have little say in classroom procedures (basic), then the facilitator may feel undervalued, resulting in tension between the teacher and facilitator. Students will quickly catch on and their learning will be compromised. When the facilitator feels comfortable providing input that is often implemented (proficient) or even invited to work with the teacher to brainstorm and implement effective strategies together (accomplished), student learning will not be compromised.

Student Behavior/Academic Concerns

As mentioned before, even in the virtual classroom, behavior issues may still occur. Academic concerns will inevitably also be an issue for some students. The teacher and facilitator must work together to address these concerns. Here is an overview of what that relationship looks like in regards to student behavior/academic issues:

- Teacher does not bring issues up and leaves them to the facilitator: Unsatisfactory
- Teacher only discusses issues when the facilitator brings them up: Basic
- Teacher usually reaches out to the facilitator to address issues: Proficient
- Teacher and facilitator routinely discuss issues and work together to solve them: Accomplished

Indicator 4C: Student Engagement & Motivation

A high-quality virtual learning environment requires the teacher to consider student interest and abilities when planning instruction. The teacher must also create common class goals and individualized student goals that include pathways to success and access to online resources based on each student's ability. Furthermore, the teacher must provide multiple opportunities for students to interact with each other and the teacher. There are three Strands that contribute to student engagement and motivation.

Goal-Setting

Goal-setting in the classroom allows students to understand expectations and purpose. This helps students stay motivated when challenges arise and engaged in having an active part in their learning outcomes. When in a virtual classroom, goals can easily be placed in the LMS and should include online activities. When students don't have goals (unsatisfactory) or the goals are generally forgotten once created and not visible in the LMS (basic), then student engagement and motivation can suffer. But, if student goals are clearly placed in the students' LMS and modified with the lessons, it can often drive class discussions and are frequently referenced (proficient) or even further supported through teacher motivation, suggestions, and opportunities to reach goals (accomplished), then students will likely experience success and have positive learning outcomes. Accomplished teachers also incorporate student goals into their lesson plans and remember each student's goals to align to their assignments.

Lessons

The art of teaching allows teachers to infuse creativity and originality into what can sometimes be dry lessons. When lessons are standard textbook lessons with outdated or irrelevant topics, most of which are PDFs and are not modified for the virtual learning environment (unsatisfactory), student engagement will clearly wane. If the students have some materials virtually, but nothing has been developed for the LMS for students to follow, go back to, engage with during & after class, and all homework has to be scanned instead of being completed virtually (basic), then again, we lose student motivation and will likely experience reduced classroom success. However, if lesson interest is immediate, students have access to most materials electronically in the LMS, and expectations have been set that the lesson will use virtual resources, but interest slowly tapers due to lack of connection to the real world or other learning (proficient), the teacher is on the right track, but still not optimizing student learning. It is only when student interest is consistent throughout the lesson due to creative ways to capture attention AND interest is maintained because of real-life/personal connections followed by a dynamic virtual classroom that has every lesson connected in the LMS with no static materials (accomplished) that student engagement has been maximized, paving the way for success in the classroom. The accomplished teacher spends extra time creating unique materials online for students to use virtually to drive engagement during every class lesson.

Praise/Recognition

Most people appreciate acknowledgment for a job well done. Not only do we feel a sense of accomplishment, but we feel a sense of recognition. For students who are developing their sense of intellect, praise can go a long way. The following levels of praise are based on the proficiency level of the teacher:

- Praise is limited to simple affirmations (e.g., "Way to go," "Good job," and "Nice"): Unsatisfactory
- Praise includes extra credit and educational games (e.g., using Kahoot, or five extra points on a quiz): Basic
- Praise is targeted to student interests (e.g., the facilitator shared students like the local college football team, so they all get pencils with the school's logo): Proficient
- Praise is tailored to student interests using a survey to determine unique awards (e.g., a spiderman coloring book for a spidey-fan, lunch with the teacher for the student who values quality time, etc.): Accomplished

Short Story: Accomplished Leader from the Virtual Classroom,
Ms. Loren, Instructional Coach

Knowing your students is the key to building a rapport and making connections with them. Making a connection is the single most important thing a teacher needs to do with their students. They can do interest inventories or intrest surveys in the beginning of the year with their students to get to know them. This proves especially important when working with some of our disaffected/unmotivated youth. Some teachers just mentioning an upcoming football game or club meeting in school may spark interest in a child. Other times, knowing a student's interests can help a teacher or counselor establish a reward system to get a student motivated.

It is the teacher's responsibility to work with the high achieving students to avoid hitting a plateau and to continue challenging them, while at the same time, also working with struggling students in getting them to grow as well. Setting individual goals and expectations is important. For example, in a writing portfolio, a student's goals may be put in and then both the teacher and student monitor progress . The goal is for the student to achieve the goal by self-monitoring and self-reflection on their progress. During teacher-student conferencing, the goals should be discussed and adjusted as needed. As goals are attained, new goals are to be added and worked towards.

Another technique accomplished teachers use is peer conferencing and peer-editing. Students utilize a rubric to score their peers' work giving specific examples of why they scored something as they did. The rubric should be student-friendly and concrete, not vague and subjective. In the peer conference, students give some suggestions for their classmates to improve their work and also give some positive feedback about the work. This leads to more student self-monitoring and them becoming self-regulated learners.

Teachers are able to host class meetings daily on platforms such as Google Meet, Microsoft Teams, or Zoom. Within these large groups, teachers are able to create subsets or small breakout rooms for collaborative group activities or discussions. The teacher can monitor the discussion going from group to group as the host. They can also utilize the chat feature to get student feedback and input as they work on attaining the completion of the assignment.

Teachers have had to be creative in how they are reaching and connecting with their kids virtually. Educators across America have worked to establish rapport and build relationships and connections daily. From using a chat feature, to annotating student work, to interactive engagement and thought-provoking lessons, educators are building positive relationships with students.

Indicator 4D: Teacher Support & Availability

Students need to know their teachers are there for them. Students also need clear and consistent content delivery to make the most of their classroom time. This indicator evaluates how supportive and accommodating the teacher is. From grading to tech-issues to student needs, does the teacher put forth an effort to create the most effective learning environment? Let's take a look at a couple of examples within this indicator.

Audio

Imagine sitting in an in-person classroom and seeing the teacher's mouth move, but not hearing a word. The entire lesson would be lost. Now, imagine sitting in a virtual classroom and the teacher's mouth is moving, but no words are coming out. What would you do? As a teacher, ensuring the students can hear you is a fundamental part of your job. An unsatisfactory rating would be given when students cannot hear the majority of the lesson and the teacher makes no effort to resolve the issue. A basic rating would be given when students often do not hear a large part of the lesson and the teacher makes minimal effort to resolve issues. In the proficient teacher's classroom, students always hear all of the lesson and if a rare audio issue occurs, the teacher immediately addresses it and revisits the parts of the lesson that were not heard. An accomplished teacher knows to check all audio/video before class and routinely checks in with students to ensure they can hear 100% of the lesson.

Meetings

Being available for students demonstrates genuine interest in their learning success. When a teacher continually misses virtual parent conferences or meetings (unsatisfactory) or is only available some of the time and requires others to meet around their schedule (basic), they give the impression that they are not truly invested in the success of their students. However, when the teacher is usually available for conferences and usually accommodates the schedules of others (proficient) and is proactive in scheduling accommodating times (accomplished), then students and parents believe the teacher is committed. They are actually going out of their way to discuss student progress and offer support for families.

Activity Set: Virtual Learning Environment & Affect

1.   Plot how you believe students perceive you AND plot how you see yourself on the scale below:

|_____|_____|

angry/bitter   indifferent   joyful

2.   If you have a facilitator, think of at least three procedures you will request his/her help on developing

_____

_____

_____

3.   S.M.A.R.T. goals are specific, measurable, achievable, relevant, and time-bound. Draft one class goal and one individual student goal for a mid-level student.

Class:_____

_____

_____

Student:_____

_____

_____

4.   Craft a plan for learning the interests of your students that can translate to recognition/incentives. Be creative so you don't

have to spend money shipping items and purchasing goodies. For example, virtual lunch with the teacher, virtual class read aloud, dress-up day, pick a new background day, etc.

How you will learn their interests:

_____

_____

_____

_____

_____

Free & Creative incentives:

_____

_____

_____

_____

5.   How will you hold yourself accountable for checking audio/video before every lesson? How will you build audio/video checks into your lesson?

_____

_____

NOTES:

Domain 5: Professional Practices & Responsibilities

Domain 5 addresses the importance of the teacher effectively participating in and completing the required responsibilities as outlined in school policy. In order to evaluate the professional practice and responsibilities, this domain focuses on two strands, with a total of seven indicators:

Strand: Class/School Responsibilities

A: Grading

B. Advanced Planning

C. Communication with Facilitator

Strand: Professional Practices

D. Relationships with Peers & Colleagues

E. Respectful Use of Social Media

F. Participation in Team & Faculty Meetings

G. Dress and Presentation

Domain 5 is evaluated according to the following examples:

- Consistently fails to meet criteria: Unsatisfactory
- Inconsistently meets criteria: Basic
- Consistently meets criteria: Proficient
- Maintains consistency and exceeds criteria: Accomplished

This means rather than exploring the examples as we did in the previous four domains, this section will evaluate the critical criteria as listed.

Indicator 5A: Grading

A teacher's approach to grading can significantly contribute to a student's self-esteem, confidence, and self-fulfilling prophecy as it relates to academic achievement. Students need feedback and the opportunity to improve their grades through continued practice. They also deserve to know their grades in a timely manner, allowing them to review material while it is still recent. Evaluating this indicator reviews three main Strands as they relate to grading.

Timeliness

Adhering to the school's grading policy is required at a minimum. If a student's assignment is not graded in LMS within two weeks, remain ungraded, or have very graded assignments (unsatisfactory), then the student is coasting through a course with relatively no benchmark for their performance. When assignments are graded within one week or there are few graded assignments (basic), students still are in the dark when it comes to their overall performance. It makes it difficult for students to plan assignments, study, and set goals for grades when they do not know where they stand. When grading deadlines are met and most assignments are graded within 72 hours, with several graded assignments (proficient), students are aware of their performance and can adequately plan a course of action to attain the grade they want. An accomplished teacher will almost always grade assignments in LMS within 48 hours combined with a wide variety of graded assignments.

Feedback

We all want to know how we're doing. Students are no different. They want to know if they met expectations for an "A" or if they "just passed." Students want to know if they are on course for the semester they planned for themselves. They also want to know if they understand the material like they think they do. Have you ever worked on something thinking it was a total breeze only to find out you left out a major Strand or you were so far off-base it would be easier to just start over? These things happen, especially when learning something new. Students deserve a teacher who will offer timely and constructive feedback to help avoid hours or days of lost time and frustration. A teacher who does not provide feedback on the LMS would earn an unsatisfactory rating. A teacher who may provide some feedback for 1-2 assignments and is generally unconstructive would earn a basic rating. A proficient teacher provides relevant feedback on several assignments and an accomplished teacher provides relevant and constructive feedback on several assignments through LMS/VDS.

Opportunities to Improve

Sometimes we just need a do-over. We thought we gave it our best and it simply wasn't enough. Maybe we knew we didn't do a great job, but hoped nobody would notice. Sometimes life happens and students need an opportunity to try again. Offering the opportunity to try again is not a sign of being weak or enabling poor behavior, rather it can be a beautiful learning moment. A time where your fallibility means you try again and not let defeat define you. Teachers must be encouraging and supportive while allowing students to experience the satisfaction of accomplishing something after many challenges. Teachers who do not provide opportunities to improve grades with multiple assignments/attempts (unsatisfactory) or who provide few opportunities to improve their grades with multiple assignments/attempts (basic) can contribute to the idea that learning is impossible for certain students. Proficient teachers often provide additional learning opportunities and Accomplished teachers not only frequently provide multiple opportunities to improve their grades, but students are aware of options ahead of time allowing them to plan their course of action.

Indicator 5B: Advanced Planning

It is expected that teachers provide two weeks of clear lesson plans accessible in the LMS that are relevant to identified student levels and aligned with the class syllabus. Advanced planning is important for a few reasons. First and most obvious, if the teacher experiences an emergency and will be absent unexpectedly, a substitute must be able to follow the virtual class plan in the LMS to mitigate any lost instructional time. Additionally, keeping plans two weeks in advance can help the teacher understand what is coming next in the lesson and makes it easier to build upon student learning with an ultimate goal in mind. This also allows for the teacher to better build a tiered virtual classroom by assigning additional lessons for the students that are advancing at a faster pace in class. Finally, allowing students access to the advanced planning material can help them make connections regarding expectations and sequential learning. Here is how teachers will be evaluated as it relates to Advanced Planning:

- Lesson plans are not available and are being created immediately before or during class (if at all), not accessible to students in the LMS, and unrelated to current topics and student levels: Unsatisfactory

- Lesson plans are generally basic and for less than two weeks; they mostly contain unrelated material and student levels; might be accessible in the LMS, but do not allow for any type of tiered classroom environment: Basic

- Lesson plans are effective and cover two week with clear materials/assignments and are accessible to students in the LMS; they mostly contain plans related to current material; allow for the teacher to provide access to content for different learning styles and speeds: Proficient

- Lesson plans are in-depth, effective, and cover three to four weeks with clear, detailed instructions and are accessible to all students in the LMS; the content is related to current material and tailored to student levels before the students even gain access, so a true tiered classroom environment exists: Accomplished

Indicator 5C: Communication with Facilitator (optional)

Although we addressed how to best utilize a facilitator in the virtual classroom, if you are fortunate enough to have a facilitator, we have not addressed the expectations regarding how you communicate with them. If you do not have a facilitator, you may skip to 5D. Facilitators deserve acknowledgment and should be treated as a professional.

Frequency

Teachers rated as unsatisfactory never or rarely contact the facilitator and if they respond, it is not in a timely manner. Teachers rated as basic occasionally contact the facilitator and/or may have delays in responses. Teachers rated as proficient will regularly contact the facilitator and respond in a timely manner, while accomplished teachers have continual contact with the facilitator and respond promptly.

Topics

The facilitator is there to support student learning, so when that is not the focus of the conversation, they are not being utilized properly. For example, if the teacher does not discuss student or class issues including grading/class policies/events (unsatisfactory) or discusses some issues but is largely dismissive of the facilitator's role in class (basic), then working as a team becomes more difficult. However, if the teacher discusses students and class issues and acknowledges the role of the facilitator (proficient) then they can approach classroom management, instruction, and behavior on a unified front. Furthermore, if the teacher invites the facilitator in for discussions about students and the class, then uses that feedback and acknowledges their role (accomplished), then again this powerful team will make the most of the virtual learning environment.

Professionalism

Facilitators support student learning and are respected educators. If inappropriate and unprofessional language or tone is used towards them, a teacher will receive an unsatisfactory rating. If inappropriate language or tone occurs occasionally, they may receive a basic rating. The proficient and accomplished teachers always use professional and respectful language and tone. An accomplished teacher spends time working with the facilitator outside of class to help train them on how to help teach the concepts in the upcoming lessons so they become an extension of the teacher. This enhances the learning experience for students by giving them access to two instructors during the class time and especially when in groups.

Indicator 5D: Relationship with Peers & Colleagues

Similarly to how we work with and address our facilitators specifically, we must approach our other peers and colleagues with the same level of professionalism, even in a virtual setting. This indicator evaluates a teacher's ability to have a positive, professional, and respectful attitude when interacting with peers. It is also about utilizing resources when shared and providing resources for others.

Interactions

Teachers with negative interactions and communication styles who focus on problems rather than solutions may be very difficult to work with and would earn an unsatisfactory rating, especially if they never email colleagues, join planned virtual meetings, or post in discussion boards. Teachers who sometimes join meetings and post in discussion boards, but are negative in interaction and communication with peers or show no real depth in their responses may earn a basic rating. Proficient teachers are consistently active on email, attend all virtual meetings, and respond quickly on discussion boards with positive feedback that focuses on solutions rather than problems. The accomplished teacher is consistently leading discussions & setting up virtual topics, posts solutions with in-depth answers & video examples from their classes, shares with peers positive activities & lesson plans that have worked with their students, and becomes a real leader when interacting with peers, helping everyone to raise their quality of instruction.

Resources

Peers can be great resources if you are willingly to work collaboratively and learn from each other. Those who always ignore and refuse to help or request help from others (unsatisfactory) or often do little to assist others or request support (basic) are not maximizing peer relationships. Proficient teachers accept help and offer to help others through video clips, access to their lesson plans, sharing success stories, and oftentimes by providing directions to resources. Accomplished teachers seek help from others and enthusiastically help others by providing resources, inviting them to join their classes, and providing full access to their curricular resources.

Short story: Accomplished Consultant, Mike, Child First Consulting

Mike, Sheila, and Robert work as education consultants at Child First Consulting. They are known at their firm as the Dream Team because of their high rate of success. They partner with local schools in Los Angeles and provide teachers with instructional strategies that help them meet the academic needs of their students. Mike, a burly man with a deep bellowing voice focuses on teachers at the high school level. Sheila works with middle school teachers and Robert consults with elementary teachers. Mike is their team lead and has been working with the firm for 10 years. Mike has weekly meetings with Sheila and Robert to discuss strategies and implementation strategies for their clients. Sheila is the glue of the team. She is known for her outgoing personality and loud shrieks before she laughs hysterically.

Robert is the driver of the team, known for his no-nonsense attitude, stern face, and lack of personality. Mike is old-school, goal-oriented and always implements strategies with the end in mind.

The Dream Team had been plugging along until their business was hit hard by COVID-19. The trio, who had become accustomed to working closely with one another, now had to work in isolation. Mike worried about their productivity and comradery. Sheila had gone from the life of the party to Negative Nancy. She complained about everything because she lost her ability to connect with people in person. Mike noticed Robert was still being his usual worker bee self and did not seem to be affected by the changes to their work environment. Mike asked Robert how he was able to remain effective even though their business had been drastically impacted by the pandemic. Robert helped Mike understand that work can be conducted in any environment, but they needed to have good processes in place to ensure success.

Mike scheduled their next team meeting on the virtual platform, Zoom. He was skeptical about their effectiveness while using a virtual platform, but found out his team was just as effective in a virtual environment. He assigned specific goals, benchmarks, and strategies for everyone. Mike also assigned specific tasks to each member of the team to make sure they met their clients' needs. The most important thing Mike did was institute time for the team to laugh and talk about events in their personal lives during virtual happy hours. Sheila was shrieking loudly again because she was able to maintain her personal connection with her teammates. These steps allowed the Dream Team to continue to meet the needs of their clients while enjoying the time they spent together virtually. The team was just as effective while working in a virtual environment because Mike obtained buy-in from his team, listened to the needs of his stakeholders, and established clear expectations for everyone, including himself. The Dream Team had become more effective because COVID-19 forced them to assess their processes and develop a client-centered approach.

Indicator 5E: Respectful Use of Social Media

Social media can absolutely be used as a tool for engagement, communication, and maintaining contact with friends and family. However, teachers are held to a higher standard when utilizing social media. Social media can unfortunately be misused and result in terrible consequences for teachers and students. As an educator, it is important that you are aware of best practices and you adhere to social media policies from your school/district at a minimum.

Professionalism

A teacher may never use social media to criticize their employer, other teachers/staff members, and especially not students (unsatisfactory). Even if a teacher is slightly critical of the school, peers, or students (basic), that may be a means to justify termination. A proficient teacher is mostly respectful toward their employer, peers, and students on social media and an accomplished teacher is always respectful to all stakeholders and students on social media.

Privacy

This is another category that is not just evaluated for your proficiency as a teacher, but if violated, may be cause for termination. Student privacy and confidentiality is of utmost importance for educators. If a teacher violates privacy by openly disclosing names and/or photos of peers or students (unsatisfactory) not only will they be penalized on the rubrics, but their job may be on the line. It is not recommended that teachers refer to students by name or other identifying characteristics online (basic). Proficient teachers do not disclose student names, but may reference the class in a social media post. Accomplished teachers do not disclose names or identifying information about students on social media.

Student/Family Communication

It might seem easy to create a group on Facebook or post a class schedule on Instagram, but communication with families should be limited to formal methods only. It is unsatisfactory for a teacher to contact and regularly communicate with current students and/or parents through social media. Communicating with parents and students on social media occasionally would earn a basic rating. Proficient and accomplished teachers keep communication with students and families limited to official channels (e.g., work email and phone calls).

Indicator 5F: Participation in Team & Faculty Meetings

Active participation in team meetings is vital to growing as an educator. Attending live sessions of team meetings and faculty sessions is only the first step. Once in the meetings, actively participating in activities and contributing to brainstorming sessions or problem-solving breakouts not only supports individual growth, but also adds value to the rest of the team.

Contributions

Some people might try to hide in the background or lay low. Sometimes they are underprepared and don't want to seem unaware of the topic, sometimes they need time to process and don't want to speak too soon, and other times they are genuinely uninterested in the meeting and have checked out. Whatever the reason is, teachers are encouraged to create a plan of action for themselves that allows for active participation in every meeting. Whether that means preparing what you plan to say the night before or finding one area that you can speak on with authentic interest. If a teacher never or rarely contributes ideas and/or responses during VDS (unsatisfactory) or occasionally contributes one or two ideas (basic), this teacher is not adding much value for their peers and also not engaging in their own learning. On the other hand, a proficient teacher often contributes several ideas and an accomplished teacher always contributes many ideas and often recommends meeting topics.

Professionalism

We've covered this in a few other sections already, but it merits notice here as well. Peers can tell when someone is begrudgingly attending a meeting. You may forget your camera is on when you roll your eyes or that you're unmuted when you speak out of turn. Being a professional during virtual meetings is critical in building solid relationships with colleagues and acting in the best interest of your team. Always using disrespectful language and unprofessional tone during discussions (unsatisfactory) or mostly using disrespectful language and unprofessional tone during discussions (basic) is not acceptable as an educator. Proficient teachers are respectful and professional during discussions and accomplished teachers are not only respectful and professional, but also actively listen and encourage others.

Application of Information/Resources

A meeting is only as good as the implemented results. Words without action will not benefit students, so we need teachers who are willing to implement the outcomes of the meetings they attend. Teachers with an unsatisfactory rating do not use information/resources received in meetings while teachers with a basic rating may apply some information/resources. Proficient teachers apply information/resources received in meetings while accomplished teachers not just apply it, but build upon the information/resources.

Short Story: An Accomplished Teacher from the Virtual Classroom, Sarah, Biology Department Chair

Sarah is a biology department chair who leads a team of teachers ranging in experience from 3-15 years and she has been teaching for eight years. Sarah calls her team the "Evil Geniuses" because they always have great ideas but constantly want to pushback against norms. Bill has been teaching biology for 10 years. He is extremely knowledgeable but does not like to share ideas with his teammates. Matt has been teaching biology for three years and has great ideas, but struggles to implement them during his classes. Mary has been teaching biology for 15 years, but does not want to participate with the team because she thinks Matt is a know-it-all and Bill is a jerk because he will not help the team. Mary also wants to make her life as easy as possible because she realizes she will need to babysit the team if she engages during team meetings.

Sarah started their professional learning team (PLT) meeting by discussing ways to create team lesson plans and common assessments to ensure their kids were mastering concepts at a high level. Bill gave her the death stare. Matt quickly stated he would write all the lesson plans for the team. Mary sighed and said this too shall pass. She pulled out a stack of papers and began grading them. Sarah shook her head and asked everyone to take a breath. Mary sighed even louder. Bill glared at Mary. Matt was oblivious to all of this because he was thinking about their lesson plans for next week.

Sarah asked everyone to discuss what they were feeling at that exact moment. Bill told the team Matt was not ready to implement his lesson plans and Mary did not care. Mary said she did care but she was not interested in changing her teaching style. Sarah spent the next 15 minutes getting the team to state their pros and cons for having common lesson plans and assessments. Everyone agreed this could be a good strategy and it could make their lives easier if they were on the same page. They also agreed they did not understand their teammates' instructional strategies.

Sarah asked the team to share one thing their teammates did well. Matt stated Bill was extremely knowledgeable. He also stated Mary had more experience and understood the needs of their students. Bill told Sarah that she was good at getting the team to focus on common goals. Bill also agreed Mary was great with student engagement. Mary, who was still trying to grade papers, looked up and told Bill she appreciated the compliment. She asked Sarah how they could implement common lessons.

They spent the next 45 minutes organizing their curriculum for the remainder of the semester. They broke their curriculum down into four areas and agreed to each write plans for one of the four areas. The team met the following week to review and approve their plans. They began to implement Sarah's idea for team lesson plans and common assessments. The team met one month later to review their data from each common assessment. The team agreed their students were more focused and achieving mastery at a higher level. The team also came to meetings ready to work with less distractions.

Sarah's idea of common lesson plans and assessments focused the group and allowed them to become more effective. Every team member worked more efficiently because they felt valued and had distinguished roles with expected outcomes.

Indicator 5G: Dress & Presentation

It might seem easier to not fully prepare in the morning when you are teaching in a virtual environment. However, online teachers are still professionals and should conduct themselves as such. Students deserve the respect that comes with properly presenting yourself as a professional who is responsible for conveying knowledge and setting high standards, both academically and personally. Here is a summary of how dress and presentation will be evaluated:

- Wrinkled or stained clothing that is not employer prescribed; disheveled appearance that may cause a distraction or contribute to unprofessionalism: Unsatisfactory
- Business or business casual clothing that is not employer prescribed; may sometimes appear disheveled or unprofessional: Basic
- Wears employer-issued clothing for most classes or may occasionally wear a similar style/color shirt; appearance in neat and professional: Proficient
- Wears employer prescribed clothing for all live classes and related meetings; appearance is neat, professional, and complimentary to virtual teaching

---

Activity Set: Professional Practices & Responsibilities

1.   How do you plan on staying updated on school policies? Brainstorm at least three ways you can remain current with possible policy updates.

_____

_____

_____

2.   What will be your biggest challenge when trying to do advanced planning? How will you overcome that challenge? Challenge:

_____

_____

Solution:

_____

_____

3.   Not everyone's personalities click all of the time. How can you ensure you will treat your facilitator/ peers/colleagues with respect even when you find them annoying/frustrating?

_____

_____

_____

4.   List all of your social media accounts. What strategy will you use for each one of them to ensure current students do not connect with you? Consider using nicknames and enhanced privacy search features.

_____

_____

5.   Team and faculty meetings can be filled with information, updates, activities, and resources. Create an online folder where you can house these resources for quick reference when you need them. Be intentional about sorting resources. Consider creating separate folders for content areas, grade levels, behavior, communication, reference documents, reporting templates, etc.

NOTES:

Synthesizing the Learning

We covered five domains intended to set the standard for high-quality virtual instruction. At a high level, these domains included:

1. Home Instructional Space & Technology

2. Class Preparation

3. Content Knowledge & Virtual Instruction

4. Virtual Learning Environment & Affect

5. Professional Practices & Responsibilities

Excelling as a virtual educator does not happen by exceeding in any one domain, but in understanding how they tie together. Excellence in education does not occur in a vacuum, rather is part of a holistic approach in ensuring student learning is at the center of all that we do as educators.

The virtual classroom has opened so many doors for students. From issues of access to personalized learning to dynamic formative assessments, online learning is absolutely the solution many students needed. However, it can also pose as a great impediment for educators who are uncomfortable or unfamiliar with the technology. Immersing yourself in the technological capabilities of a virtual classroom is imperative in ensuring you are maximizing instructional time while meeting student needs.

We are on the cutting edge of innovative technology that allows us to serve students in ways never before possible. Not only are you making a difference, but you are making history. You are also engaging in your own learning. Just as we would address student frustrations, apply those same strategies to yourself when technology throws you for a loop. Recognize you are learning and a few failures are expected in the process. What's more important than messing up is how you respond. Do you allow resilience to take over as you remind yourself, "You've got this!" or do you wallow in your frustration and decide to quit trying. Learning from our mistakes helps us become better educators and more importantly, better people. There will undoubtedly be a moment where it feels like things are falling apart or not going the way you had planned, but stick with it. Learn from it. Be better because of it.

Here's the reality- you're not just doing this for your own personal growth or professional gain, you are doing this for those eager learners on the other side of your screen. You have a classroom full of people who rely on you to teach them, guide them, give them course credits, and mold their academic career. You mean so much to them and your ability to persevere when your evaluator seems tough or when your internet flickers is more influential than you know.

When you were going through each domain, there may have been one or two that stood out to you as more challenging than the rest. We encourage you to revisit those sections and read more about the examples and critical criteria in the downloadable rubrics at virtualteacherassociation.org. Jot down your questions and areas of clarification. Email peers or advisors on their perception of your proficiency level in that domain or indicator. Approach these challenges with an open mind and be prepared for constructive criticism. Avoid emotionally-tied responses because at the end of the day, this feedback will help you become a better teacher. Be willing to release ideas that are holding you back and accept suggestions that may propel you further. You are on a growth journey as a virtual educator and we want it to feel positive and productive. We believe in you and the difference you are making.

Resources

Check out these additional resources on our website, virtualteacherassociation.org, as you explore more opportunities to grow as a virtual educator:

- Free Professional Development Course: Best Practices for Online Instruction

- Certification Course: $599 to earn certification as a highly-qualified virtual instructor

- Certification Course + Graduate Credit: $764 to earn certification as a highly-qualified virtual instructor AND three graduate credits through Adams State University

- Training of Trainers: Inquire about in-person training for a group of up to 12 leaders at your organization on virtual instruction best practices

Notes:

Made in the USA
Monee, IL
01 November 2020

46456231R00073